Book br

1. This novel by Daniel Defoe, 1719, is considered one of the first examples of the English novel and was an immediate success, both in England and then abroad.

2. Set in the middle of the 17th century, Robinson Crusoe an Englishman, tells the story of his adventures at sea and then the 28 years he spends on a deserted island.

3. Robinson Crusoe has many problems on the island at first, but he soon learns to make things grow, to build for himself, and to live a good life.

4. Defoe probably based part of *Robinson Crusoe* on the life of a real person, Alexander Selkirk, a Scottish sailor who lived on a deserted island from 1704 to 1709.

5. This novel is also considered the start of realistic fiction as a literary genre. Indeed, at first, many people thought Robinson Crusoe was a real person.

www.eligradedreaders.com

In this reader:

21st Century Skills	To encourage students to connect the story to the world they live in.
Movers	A1 level activities.
Culture notes	Brief cultural information.
Glossary	An explanation of difficult words.
Picture Caption	A brief explanation of the picture.
Audio	These icons indicate the parts of the story that are recorded: start ▶ stop ■

The FSC certification guarantees that the paper used in these publications comes from certified forests, promoting responsible forestry management worldwide.

For this series of ELI graded readers, we have planted 5000 new trees.

Daniel Defoe

Robinson Crusoe

Retold and Activities by
Silvana Sardi

Illustrated by
Matteo Berton

Young Adult ΞΗ Readers

Young Adult Eli Readers

The **ELI Readers** collection is a complete range of books and plays for readers of all ages, ranging from captivating contemporary stories to timeless classics. There are four series, each catering for a different age group: **First ELI Readers**, **Young ELI Readers**, **Teen ELI Readers** and **Young Adult ELI Readers**. The books are carefully edited and beautifully illustrated to capture the essence of the stories and plots. The readers are supplemented with 'Focus on' texts packed with background cultural information about the writers and their lives and times.

Robinson Crusoe
Daniel Defoe
Retold and Activities
Silvana Sardi

Illustrations
Matteo Berton

ELI Readers
Founder and Series Editors
Paola Accattoli, Grazia Ancillani, Daniele Garbuglia (Art Director)

Graphic Design
Tiziana Barigelletti

Production Manager
Francesco Capitano

Photo credits
Shutterstock, ELI Archive
© **New edition: 2022**
First edition: 2015
ELi, Gruppo editoriale ELi
P.O. Box 6
62019 Recanati (MC)
Italy
T +39 071750701
F +39 071977851
info@elionline.com
www.elionline.com

*Typeset in 10,5 / 15 pt Monotype Fulmar
Printed in Italy by Tecnostampa – Pigini Group Printing Division
Loreto – Trevi (Italia) – ERA 111.10*

ISBN 978-88-536-3224-1

www.eligradedreaders.com

Contents

6	Main Characters	
8	Before you read	
10	Chapter 1	A New Life
18	Activities	
20	Chapter 2	The Island
28	Activities	
30	Chapter 3	Learning New Things
38	Activities	
40	Chapter 4	Savages
48	Activities	
50	Chapter 5	Friday
58	Activities	
60	Chapter 6	Going Home
70	Activities	
72	Focus on...	Daniel Defoe
74	Focus on...	CLIL History: Atlantic Slave Trade
76	Focus on...	Robinson Crusoe in the 20th and 21st Centuries
78	Test yourself	
79	Syllabus	

MAIN

ROBINSON CRUSOE

He tells the story of this adventures at sea and his life on a desert island.

ROBINSON'S FATHER

A merchant, he wants Robinson to find a good job and stay at home.

ROBINSON'S MOTHER

She's from a good English family. She doesn't want Robinson to travel the seas.

CHARACTERS

XURY

A slave boy who is with Crusoe in Sallee, Africa.

PORTUGUESE CAPTAIN

He helps Robinson in Africa and takes him to Brazil.

FRIDAY

A Caribbean native, he becomes Robinson's slave on the island.

Before you Read

Vocabulary

1 Choose a word from the box to put under each picture. Use a dictionary to help you. You will find all these words in *Robinson Crusoe*.

> pirate • island • sand • wave • raft • gun • hammock • sail • hill • cave • goat • basket • umbrella • savage • grapes • turtle • grain

PEOPLE

1 p _ _ _ _ _

2 s _ _ _ _ _

NATURE

3 i _ _ _ _ _

4 s _ _ _

5 w _ _ _

6 h _ _ _

7 c _ _ _

THINGS

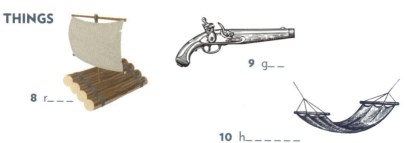

8 r _ _ _

9 g _ _

10 h _ _ _ _ _ _

11 s_ _ _   12 b_ _ _ _ _   13 u_ _ _ _ _ _ _

ANIMALS

14 g_ _ _   15 t_ _ _ _ _

FOOD

16 g_ _ _ _   17 g_ _ _ _ _

Listening

2 Listen and choose the right answer, A, B or C about Chapter One.

0 Robinson's father was from
   A ☐ England.
   B ☑ Germany.
   C ☐ Scotland.

1 In Hull, Robinson's father bought
   A ☐ a house.
   B ☐ a wife.
   C ☐ a boat.

2 His mother was from
   A ☐ Germany.
   B ☐ England.
   C ☐ America.

3 Robinson had
   A ☐ three sons.
   B ☐ three brothers.
   C ☐ two brothers.

4 Robinson didn't want to
   A ☐ leave his town.
   B ☐ find a job in his town.
   C ☐ travel.

5 Robinson wanted to see the world
   A ☐ by road.
   B ☐ by sea.
   C ☐ in books.

6 One morning, he spoke to his father
   A ☐ in his bedroom.
   B ☐ in his bathroom.
   C ☐ in the living room.

7 His father wanted to help him
   A ☐ buy a fast ship.
   B ☐ find a good wife.
   C ☐ find a good job.

Chapter One

A New Life

▶ 2　My name is Robinson Crusoe and I want to tell you about my life. My father was German but came to live and work in Hull, England. He made lots of money with his business and bought a nice house. Then, he met my mother. She came from a good English family called Robinson, and soon they were husband and wife. I came into this world in 1632. Now they had three sons and they called me Robinson. At that time, my family name was 'Kreutznaer'. After many years in England, everybody started to call us 'Crusoe'.

In the 17th century, the most important merchants in Hull sent most of their goods to Holland.

My first brother died and nobody knows anything about my other brother. He went out one day and never came back. My father was very old. He often asked:

'Robinson, my son, will you stay here, please and find a job near home?'

Every time he asked, I didn't answer. My father understood that I wanted to leave my town. He was very sad. I was a good student but I wanted to stop studying and see the world. I didn't want a job at a desk. I wanted to travel the seas and make lots of money.

My father said: 'Robinson, please don't go!'

My mother said: 'Robinson, don't leave your father and I!'

My friends said: 'Robinson, stay here, where you're safe!'

Robinson Crusoe

Did I listen to them? No! It was my life and I wanted to live it!

One morning, my father called me to his room. He was in bed because he wasn't very well. I was only eighteen at the time. I looked at his tired, sad eyes and felt sorry. Again, he asked me to stay at home.

'You don't have to travel the seas to make money,' he said. 'I'll help you find a good job. You'll have a great life here.'

'But father,' I said, 'it's not only for the money. I want to see the world. Can't you understand? I love you and mother, but I have to do this.'

'But you'll have a hard life, my boy. Your life here now, is easy. You aren't rich* but you aren't poor. You've got all you need.'

'I know, but I need more,' I answered.

On 1st September 1651, I left Hull to go to London on my friend's ship*. I didn't tell my parents. There was a lot of wind and the ship went up and down, up and down. I didn't feel very well. I wanted to go home but I couldn't. I remembered my mother and father and felt sad.

The morning after the storm*, the weather was good. I forgot the difficult night before and started to enjoy my first voyage*. I was excited about seeing London. Then, there was a storm again.

'Robinson,' said my friend, 'we have to leave the ship, it's going down! Come with me. There's a small boat we can use!'

With the small boat, we got to Yarmouth. Here, my friend's father said to me:

'Young man, don't go to sea again, please! After two storms on your first voyage, can't you see it isn't the life for you? We don't want to travel with you again!'

rich with a lot of money
ship big boat

storm very bad weather with wind and rain
voyage travelling by sea

Daniel Defoe

Robinson's father is asking his son to stay at home.

I didn't answer him. I was sorry, but I wanted to go to London. I had some money and travelled to London by road. I stayed there some time and waited for a new voyage.

This time I travelled on a ship to Africa. The captain* was my friend, and I enjoyed talking to him.

He taught me lots about ships, and I was happy to learn these things. This voyage went very well.

In Africa, the people bought some small things from me, so I came back to London with some money. I stayed in London for two or three months, because my friend, the captain, died. One of his friends had a ship, so we left for Africa together. Before I left, I gave the captain's wife some of my money. I also took some money with me on the voyage. But we didn't get to Africa because pirates came and took our ship and all our money. Now, we had nothing. The captain of the pirates took me to his home in Sallee, North Africa, to be his slave* because I was young and could work hard. I thought of my father and mother and wanted to go home; I couldn't. I didn't know that this was only the first of many problems to come.

The captain of the pirates didn't take me on his voyages. He left me at home to work in his garden and in the house. It was all very boring for me. When he came home from his voyages, I had to stay on the ship and clean it. Every evening, I thought about my difficult life and how much I wanted to go home.

After about two years, the captain of the pirates stayed at home all the time because he had no money for his voyages. He liked catching fish and went out in his small boat every week. He often took me and a young boy called Xury, with him.

> The Barbary pirates were based in North Africa and they attacked ships in the Mediterranean, south along West Africa's Atlantic coast and into the North Atlantic as far north as Iceland. They took merchant ships and attacked towns on the coast to take slaves.

captain the person who is the head of a ship

slave this person has to work for other people, but he/she doesn't get any money and isn't free

One morning, we went to catch some fish. The weather was good when we left. Then, two hours later, a storm started. Before the storm, we could see the beach. After the storm, there was only the sea. It was difficult to get back to the beach and we didn't get home till late in the evening. From that day, the captain of the pirates stayed at home. When he wanted some fish, he sent me and Xury with one of his friends. One day, he invited some friends for dinner. That morning he told me:

'Go and get some fish for me. Use the big boat. My friend will go with you and Xury. Take some water and biscuits too.'

I started to think: a big boat, water, biscuits… with these things, was it possible for me to leave and never come back? I began to think about the things I needed for a long voyage. I found some tools* and put them in the boat.

We left early in the morning. There was a good wind and the boat went fast. We stopped to catch some fish. I called the captain's friend.

'Look at this big fish!' I said.

He came to see and looked into the water. I was behind him. I kicked him. The next minute, he was in the water below.

'Help! Help!' he said.

I looked at Xury. He looked at me and we were both happy. I was free*! The captain's friend swam well, but he couldn't catch us, so he swam to the beach. We never saw him again. I was so happy and excited. Xury was surprised.

I said, 'Xury, I'll take you with me, but you must be good and help me.'

tools you use these to work or make things   **free** not a slave

'Don't worry, I'll work hard for you,' said Xury.

We travelled for five days. Then one evening, we came to a little river. I wanted to look for water to drink, and waited until it was night. But then we heard the noise of animals, so we waited until morning. The animals came and swam near us. I didn't know what kind of animals they were. They were very big and there was a lot of noise. We didn't sleep that night. Morning came and Xury said:

'I'll go and look for water. Stay here on the boat where it's safe.'

'You're a good boy, but no, we'll go together,' I said.

We found clean water and didn't see any big animals. I didn't know what country we were in, only that it was Africa. We didn't meet any people, so we went back to our boat to start our voyage again. We travelled for 12 days and stopped sometimes for water. By day, we saw nothing and nobody. By night, we heard the noise of the animals. We didn't have many biscuits and I started to worry. Then, one afternoon, Xury said:

'Look! A big ship!'

'Hurrah!' I said, 'We're safe!'

It was a Portuguese ship. They took us on their ship and gave us food and water. I said I was an Englishman. I told them about the captain of the pirates. I also told them about my life when I was a slave and who Xury was.

'You're safe now, my friend,' said the Portuguese captain. 'You can travel with us. We're going to Brazil.'

'But I haven't got money to pay for the voyage,' I said.

'Don't worry, I don't want any money,' said the captain.

'Thank you, my friend,' I said.

Daniel Defoe

Robinson is looking at his ship from the beach.

The captain bought my boat from me and gave me money for Xury too. I was sorry for this, but I needed the money.

'Don't worry,' said the captain. 'The boy will be free after ten years with me.'

The voyage was fine and we got to Brazil after twenty-two days. In Brazil, a lot of people were rich because they had sugar plantations*. I bought a plantation and started to make sugar. It was a hard life and there weren't any houses with families near me. I had nobody to talk to. Sometimes, I thought my plantation was a desert* island and I felt sad. I stayed there for four years. Each year, I made a lot of sugar from my plantation and I now had a slave to help me with the work. But, I was bored and wanted to travel again. Eh? I hear you ask. What can I say? I was young… too young. Some other men had plantations. They wanted slaves to work on them.

'I'll go to Africa to get the slaves,' I said. 'Can you work on my plantation for me? I'll be back soon.'

They all said yes. I left on 1st September 1659. I was so happy to be on a ship again! I felt free!

At first, the weather was good. Then, there was a big storm for twelve days. The wind and rain drove our ship into the sand at the bottom of the sea, where it stopped. Eleven of us went into a small boat. It was early morning. A big wave came. I was in the water. I thought it was time to die, but I swam and swam. I closed my eyes… then… I was on a beach! A beach! I opened my eyes. I was safe!

plantation big farm   **desert** (here) with no people

After-Reading Activities • Chapter One

Reading

1 **Are these sentences about Chapter One right (A) or wrong (B)?**

		A	B
	Robinson Crusoe's mother was German.	☐	☑
1	His brothers weren't at home.	☐	☐
2	Robinson wanted to see the world.	☐	☐
3	After the storm, he went to London by boat.	☐	☐
4	The captain of the pirates was Robinson's friend.	☐	☐
5	The Portuguese captain took Robinson to Brazil.	☐	☐
6	Robinson had his sugar plantation for eight years.	☐	☐

Speaking - Pair Work ◆ 21st Century Skills

2 **Talk to a partner about these questions and write your answers.**

1 Which countries would you like to visit? Why?
   ....
   ....
   ....

2 Would you like to work or study in another town or city? Why?
   ....
   ....
   ....

3 What can we learn by visiting other countries?
   ....
   ....
   ....

4 What can be difficult about moving to another country?
   ....
   ....
   ....
   ....
   ....
   ....

Vocabulary

3 **Finish the sentences with a word from the box.**

> river • days • work • sugar • fish • family • business • money • life • home • world

   In Africa, Robinson had a hard ......*life*...... .

1. His father made a lot of money with his ....
2. Robinson didn't want a job near his ....
3. His mother came from a good ....
4. Robinson wanted to see the ....
5. Robinson gave the captain's wife some ....
6. One morning Robinson went to catch some ....
7. One evening, Robinson and Xury came to a little ....
8. Robinson bought a plantation and started to make ....
9. Robinson had a slave to help him with the ....
10. There was a big storm for twelve ....

Pre-Reading Activitiy • Chapter Two

Speaking

4 **At the end of Chapter One, Robinson Crusoe is on an island. Answer these questions with a friend. Then read Chapter Two, and see how many of your answers are right.**

1. Are there other people on the island?
2. Are there any animals on the island?
3. What kind of fruit is there on the island?
4. Is there any clean water to drink on the island?
5. Does Robinson like the island?
6. Can he catch fish to eat?
7. Where will he make his house?

Chapter Two

The Island

▶ 4   Where was I? What country was this? Where were the others? I looked up and down the long beach. I couldn't see anybody. I started to walk and call my friends. There was no answer. Then I saw a hat in the water, then two shoes, one black, one brown. I looked at the sea. Our ship was there. The sand below the water was its bed, but there was nobody on the ship now.

I was tired and hungry and I needed some water. I began to worry about the night. I remembered the noise of the animals at night in Africa. Were there any animals here? Did they want to eat me? Near the beach, there were some trees. Near the trees, I found some clean water to drink. Now I was very tired. I found a big tree and slept in it all night.

I woke up early next morning. It was a beautiful day. I could see the ship. There were no big waves now. I wanted to swim to the ship. There were things on the ship that I needed to live. It was hot now and it was nice to feel the cold water on my body.

I got to the ship and I went to the kitchen. Yippee! The kitchen wasn't under water. I found some biscuits. I needed a boat for all the things I wanted to take with me. I didn't have a boat, but I made a raft. I found some big boxes. I put lots of food in the first box and put it on

Robinson Crusoe

the raft. There was rice, bread, cheese, meat and some grain. Then, I found some clothes; a coat, a jacket, some shirts, trousers, shoes and a hat. I put these in a box on the raft as well.

In my third box, there were some tools. I wanted these tools to make a house or a boat or small things; a table or a chair. I also took some guns. I went back with all these things on my raft. This time I didn't stop on the beach, but went up a small river. There I stopped. Yippee! Everything was safe on the raft! Now I had lots of things to help me live. In the afternoon, I went for a walk. I wanted to find a good place to put all my things. I wanted to know: was this an island or not? I hoped not. Were there any people or not in this place? I hoped so.

I walked up and up. Phew! It was hot! Then, I stopped and looked down. There was water everywhere! I was on an island! And it was a desert island because I couldn't see any other people! I felt very sad and sat down. A desert island all for me. I could see two other small islands. They weren't very near. There were lots of birds on the island but I didn't know what kind they were. Were they good to eat? I didn't know.

The island is somewhere in South America, probably near the coast of Venezuela.

I went back down to my raft. That night, I made a kind of house with the boxes and slept there. I thought about other things I needed. I wanted to go back to the ship again. I had to go before a storm came again.

Next morning, I got up early and swam back to the ship. I took many things; other tools, clothes, a hammock and some of the ship's sails. I made a second raft and took these things back to the island.

When I got back to my boxes, there was a big cat sitting near them.

Daniel Defoe

Robinson feels safe in his house on the island.

I gave it a biscuit. It ate it, then went away. I made a little house with the sails and put all my things inside. I was happy. My things were safe now. Safe from animals and from the sun or rain. The boxes were a wall outside my house. I slept well that night after all my hard work.

I went back to the ship eleven times. Each time I took something back to the island; more bread, sugar, some knives, and parts of the ship. I found some money too. I took it but didn't know why... I couldn't use money on a desert island!

Thirteen days after I came to the island, there was a storm again. I slept safe in my little house with all my things. When I woke up the next morning, the ship wasn't there.

It was at the bottom of the sea.

I now wanted to find a different place for my house. I needed a place where there was clean water.

I didn't want a house in the sun and I wanted to be safe from animals. I also wanted a place to watch for ships at sea. I found a great place on a hill. There was a cave on this hill and I made my house there. It was safe because nobody could come down from above, and I could see everything below. The sea was in front of my house and I could watch for ships all day. I was also happy because the sun came to this part of the island in the evening. I made a wall outside my house and a sail was the door of the cave. I felt safe inside with all my things from the ship.

Robinson hoped to see ships using the triangular trade route that went from Europe to West Africa and then to the Caribbean and American colonies.

I had the hammock for my bed and I slept well at night. After all this work, I started to go out with my gun to look for food. There were a lot of animals but I didn't know which were good to eat. I also wasn't very good with a gun and many times I came home with nothing.

I walked a lot and one day I saw some goats on the island. I was very

excited. It was now possible for me to have meat. The only problem was that they were very fast and it was difficult to catch them.

I watched them for many days. They always went to the same places and I waited for them with my gun. I now had meat. I also caught a baby goat and took it home.

Sometimes I was happy because I had a house and food, but I was often very sad. I thought of my family and friends. Here, I had nobody to talk to. I never saw any ships near the island. My life was here now and I could do nothing to change it. Then I thought of my friends on the ship. They were at the bottom of the sea. I wasn't. I had tools, clothes, food and water. Life wasn't that bad after all!

After some days on the island, I made a cross with my knife on a tree for every day. I did this every morning. Oh, and I forgot to tell you about the animals. When I went to the ship to get all the things you know about, I found a dog and two cats. I took them home with me. The dog always stayed with me. He was a good friend. The cats were often outside but always came home for dinner.

It was now November. Every day, I looked for a ship at sea, but there were never any ships for me. Every day, I looked for food on the island. There were grapes and I ate a lot of them. I also made a table and a chair for my house. I used the tools from the ship. I started on Monday and finished after a week. I made the table four times before I liked it. It was the same for the chair. It wasn't easy for me, but I did it in the end. They weren't very beautiful but I thought they were great. I began to feel I had a home. Now, I could sit on my chair and eat at my table. Sometimes there was a storm with a lot of wind and rain, but I was safe in my little house.

My days were always the same. Every morning, I took my gun and went for a walk. The dog always came with me. Sometimes, with my gun, I got a bird or two. Some were good to eat, others weren't. I soon learned to remember the good birds. Then, I came home and worked until about eleven o'clock. Then I ate. After, from twelve to two, I slept because it was very hot. In the evening, I worked again. This was when I made things for the house. Then I went to bed. My hammock was my favourite thing.

The months came and went. Sometimes there was a lot of rain. Other times it was very hot. In January it was too hot to go out and I stayed at home all day. I only went out very early in the morning or late at night. I went to other parts of the island in the hills far* from the beach.

There were a lot of trees on this part of the island. Then, in one place, I found some goats. When my dog saw them, he ran back home! My baby goat at home was now big and needed a friend. I have to tell you again that goats are very difficult to catch. They run very fast up and down those hills.

After a lot of hard work, I caught two young goats and took them home. I put all three goats together near my house. They couldn't run back to the other goats because I made a big wall. I gave them food and water and they soon liked their new home. With these goats, I now had milk too! Yippee!

One day, I looked in one of my boxes and found a little bag with some seeds* inside. They were old and I didn't think they were good.

far not near   **seed** part of a plant

I put the bag outside and forgot about it. That night there was some wind. The next morning the bag wasn't there. Then, there was a lot of rain.

About a month after, I saw some long green plants coming out of the grass near my house. Then after two weeks I was excited to see that these new plants were grain. There were now also other plants. I knew these. They were rice plants. I remembered them from my time in Africa. Were these plants on other parts of the island? I looked and looked but I couldn't find any other grain or rice plants on the island. Then I remembered... the little bag with the seeds! Of course! That's where the plants came from! I was excited about having bread. But I needed a lot of grain And... how do you make bread?

It was now June. One day, I went to the beach and I found a big turtle. At that time, I didn't know that there were a lot of turtles on other parts of this island and I was very excited. I took the turtle home and cooked it. There were some eggs inside the turtle too... mmm...yummy!

That night I felt very cold. The next day I didn't feel very well. Why did I eat all that turtle? I stayed on my hammock all day. I slept a lot. I didn't eat or drink anything. I was very hot and I thought I saw my mother. Am I dying? Father! Mother! Where are you? Please, can you help me? I remembered my father's words: 'Robinson, please don't go! You'll have a hard life, my boy. Your life here now, is easy. You've got all you need.' Why do I never listen to people? Now, look at me!

I slept again. Then, after a long time, I woke up. I wasn't hot. I felt well again but it wasn't easy to walk. I was very slow. I drank some

Robinson Crusoe

water. I looked about and I was happy to see my animals, my cave and all my things. I sat outside my cave and looked at the blue sea with its white waves, the white sand of the beach, and the green of the hills and trees of the island. It was all beautiful and I felt happy to be there.

After-Reading Activities • Chapter Two

Reading

❶ Choose the right answer, A, B or C about Chapter Two.

The first night on the island, Robinson slept
- ☐ **A** on the beach.
- ☑ **B** in a tree.
- ☐ **C** on the grass.

1 In the ship's kitchen, there were
- ☐ **A** some biscuits to eat.
- ☐ **B** some coffee to drink.
- ☐ **C** some books to read.

2 Robinson put the things he found on the ship
- ☐ **A** in bags.
- ☐ **B** in boxes.
- ☐ **C** in his clothes.

3 On the island there were
- ☐ **A** lots of people.
- ☐ **B** lots of houses.
- ☐ **C** lots of birds.

4 Robinson went back to the ship
- ☐ **A** thirteen times.
- ☐ **B** eleven times.
- ☐ **C** twelve times.

5 On the ship, Robinson found
- ☐ **A** a cat and two dogs.
- ☐ **B** two cats and two dogs.
- ☐ **C** a dog and two cats.

6 For his house, Robinson made
- ☐ **A** a table and a chair.
- ☐ **B** a bed and a chair.
- ☐ **C** a bath and a chair.

7 Robinson wasn't very well
- ☐ **A** in July.
- ☐ **B** in June.
- ☐ **C** in November.

Grammar A1 MOVERS

2 **Choose the right words (A, B or C) to complete the text about Chapter Two.**

Robinson was sad when he saw that he was **(0)** .....on..... a desert island because he had nobody to talk to. He **(1)** .... to the ship many times to get everything he needed to live there. Then he **(2)** .... a house in a cave on **(3)** .... hill. Here, he could watch for ships all day and he felt safe inside his house. He started to go out with his gun to look for food **(4)** .... sometimes he didn't find anything good to eat. Then he caught **(5)** .... goats so he could have milk to drink.

0	**A** at	**B** on	**C** in
1	**A** went	**B** visited	**C** came
2	**A** did	**B** was	**C** made
3	**A** a	**B** the	**C** an
4	**A** so	**B** but	**C** because
5	**A** any	**B** no	**C** some

(B on is circled)

Pre-Reading Activity • Chapter Three

Speaking

3 **Work in pairs. Talk together and tick (✓) the things you think Robinson will learn to do in Chapter Three. Say also why.**

✓ He learns to make bread.
1 ☐ He learns to draw pictures on his walls.
2 ☐ He learns to make cheese.
3 ☐ He learns to make a boat from a tree.
4 ☐ He learns to speak a new language.
5 ☐ He learns to ride a horse.
6 ☐ He learns to make clothes.
7 ☐ He learns to make baskets.
8 ☐ He learns to make glasses.

Chapter Three

Learning New Things

▶ 5 It was the 15th July and I began to visit other parts of the island. I went up the river and I saw where the clean water came from. This was the time of year when it didn't rain much and there wasn't much water. There was grass near the river. On the hills, there were lots of plants and fruit trees. I didn't know all their names. Were they good to eat? It was difficult to tell. The grapes were good, I knew that; but the others? I also saw the sugar plant and I remembered my plantation in Brazil. The men in Brazil never got their slaves from me. I don't think they'll remember me now, I thought.

I stayed in this place all night. It was nice with all the plants there. I slept in a tree.

Next morning I walked again and saw other new parts. This part of the island was very green. I felt I was in a garden. There were lots of orange trees. Yippee, orange juice for breakfast! I wanted to take some oranges and other fruit back home to my cave, but it was very far. It was difficult to carry the fruit and when I got home after three days, all the fruit was bad and I couldn't eat it. I made a bag from one of the ship's sails and went again to this beautiful green part of my island. Yes, my island! I was the only person on it! This time I got home and the fruit was good. I looked about me when I got home. For

At the start of the 17th century, Brazil was the most important producer of sugar in the world.

a minute I thought about leaving my cave and making a new home in the beautiful garden on my island.

Then, I remembered that I could see the sea from my cave. I wanted to be near the sea to watch for any ships. The beautiful green garden wasn't near the beach. There were also all my things in the cave; my hammock, my chair, my table. It was difficult to start again from nothing. This cave was my home. But I loved my green garden and stayed there all of July. I made a second house. This time, it wasn't a cave, but a little house in the trees. I made it with parts of trees and other plants. You couldn't see it from the outside, because between the house and the green garden, there was a wall of trees. I felt safe there. Now I had a house near the sea and a house with a beautiful garden!

August came and with it, the rain. My new house wasn't good for the rain. I went back to my cave because it was good in all weather. It rained all of August, September and some of October. I stayed in my cave and ate the food I had. On the 30th September, I drew a cross on my tree. There were now three hundred and sixty five crosses on that tree; a year! I remembered when I came to this island; the storm, the big waves, then the sand under my feet. Then, I remembered my friends and I felt very sad. I needed a friend. I talked to my animals; to my dog, my cats, even to my goats, but it wasn't the same. I looked out at sea, but there was nothing. Where was I? Why were there never any ships? Didn't people travel these days? I went to bed, but I didn't sleep that night.

After all the rain, I started to work on my farm again. Yes, I now called it my farm. I had my goats, my grain and my rice, and I worked hard every day. It was important to know the right time to do things on the farm. The first time, I didn't have any grain or rice because

Daniel Defoe

Robinson understands the weather on the island now so he has lots of grain.

it didn't rain, and the plants died. Then, I began to understand the weather, the months when it rained and when there was the sun. At the start of my third year on the island, I'm happy to tell you that my plants didn't die and I had lots of grain and rice.

When the good weather came, about November, I usually went to see my other house in my garden. I called this my garden house. Everything was the same there; green and beautiful after all the rain. This is how I understood the weather on my island:

Half February
March   Rain
Half April

Half April
May
June   Sun
July
Half August

Half August
September   Rain
Half October

Half October
November
December   Sun
January
Half February

When it rained, I stayed in my house. I had food and water and I did lots of little jobs inside. I needed some baskets for my grain and other things. When I was a little boy, my father took me to town. I often watched people at work on the streets. One man made baskets and sometimes I helped him. They were beautiful. I could remember how he made them.

Near my garden house, there was a small tree. It was the right kind of tree to make baskets. I took my tools and worked hard all day on the tree. I cut* it into small, slim parts and took them back home. Then, I used these small parts to make my baskets. It was difficult at first, but I learned. Soon, I had lots of baskets for different things. They weren't beautiful but they were very useful.

Now I needed something to put water in. But what? This was a difficult problem for me. I only had some old glasses from the ship. They were very small. I also needed something to make soup in. 'I'll make these later,' I thought.

Now the weather was nice and I wanted to see the parts of the island I didn't know. I left with my gun, some tools and my dog, and started to walk. I also took some food and water. I saw my garden house. After, I could see the sea again. It was a beautiful day and I could see something... an island? I didn't know. I didn't know which part of the world I was in. Was it a part of America I could see? Who lived there? Savages? Savages ate people. I didn't want to meet any of them. I was safe here on my island. I didn't want to go to that other country.

On this part of the island, there were trees and a lot of grass and flowers. I saw a lot of parrots* too. They were all beautiful colours;

cut you do this with a knife   **parrot** a bird that can talk red, green, blue and yellow! I wanted to take a parrot home with me to my cave. I wanted to teach it to speak to me.

I waited and watched. In the end, I caught a young parrot. Later, I took it home, but it was some years before it learned to speak to me.

I enjoyed walking about the island. At night, I didn't go back to my house. I slept in a tree, then started again the next morning. I came down from the hills to the beach on this part of the island.

On my part, there weren't many turtles. Here there were hundreds! And there were a lot of different birds too. I didn't know the names of all of them, but some were very good to eat. I can say that I now had lots of different things to eat; meat, fish and fruit and I felt very well for it. This part of the island was very nice, but I had my houses and I didn't want to make a new one here too. I felt I was on holiday in this part. It wasn't my home. I enjoyed this holiday, but then it was time to go home and back to work on my farm. I was happy to sleep in my hammock again after all those nights in the trees. I could sit on my chair at my table again and have my dinner. What a great house!

I had a rest for a week, then started work again. First, I made a little house for my parrot, Poll.

I found a new place for my goats, where there was a lot of grass. I made a new wall for them. They couldn't run up the hill now. They stayed where I put them.

The 30th September came again with the rain. I remembered, for the second time, when I came to the island. Now I felt I had a good life. It was different from the first year when I didn't know anything.

In the first year, I didn't like living on this island. Now I was happy

Daniel Defoe

'A Robinson Crusoe' economy is a simple way to study economics. This model has one consumer, one producer and two goods. The name of this economy refers to what Robinson does on the island, only he's both producer and consumer.

when I woke up in the morning. I had my farm, my garden house, my animals and all the food I wanted. Now, I didn't feel sad every day, only sometimes. I was ready to start year three on the island.

I always had lots to do. I didn't have many tools and I didn't have anybody to help me. My work was slow and hard but I enjoyed it. Sometimes animals came and ate my grain. I made a wall but it wasn't easy. I started on a Saturday and finished after three weeks. This is only one example of the problems I had. Everything was difficult for me because there was only me. Then, birds came and ate my grain. I didn't know how to stop them. I needed that grain. I thought for some time. Then I got three birds with my gun. I put the dead* birds on a tree near my grain. The other birds never came back after that!

My grain was ready in December and there was a lot of it that year! I cut my grain and put it in my baskets. I did the same with my rice. I had a lot of seeds for next year. This year I needed to learn to make bread, but I didn't know where to start. The only good thing was that I had lots of time! In the next six months I made new tools to work the grain. When it rained, I stayed inside and taught my parrot to speak. The first word he said was his name, 'POLL'.

Think how excited I was when I heard him speak! It was great! After a lot of problems, I made my bread in the end. I was very happy with my work.

I also learned to make rice cakes. Every year I had all this work to do and time went fast. Sometimes I thought about the other part of the island, where I went for my 'holiday'. I thought again about the other island that was on that part. It wasn't near but... I thought

dead not living

about leaving my island. Was it safe to leave this island and go there? Were there savages on those islands? It was a difficult question to answer. I thought about Xury and the long boat we had when we left the pirate captain in Africa. I needed a boat.

'Poll, I'll make a boat from a tree!' Yes, that's what I'll do,' I said to my parrot one day. I often spoke to my parrot. It was nice for me to have somebody to talk to.

I found a tree I liked near the beach. I cut it down and started to make my boat. I was excited and worked every day. It was big and long. It was a boat for twenty-five men. I was happy when I finished it. Then… oops… how could it go into the water? It sat on the sand… my big, beautiful boat… ready for the sea, but there was a long beach between my boat and the sea and I could do nothing to get it in the water. 'Why didn't I think of this before?' I hear you ask. I know, you're right. You can learn from me… think before you do something! All that work and a boat I couldn't use!

The 30th September came again… I started my fourth year on this island. After the 'boat problem' I stopped thinking about the world outside my island. I was safe here, free from all the problems of the big world out there.

After-Reading Activities • Chapter Three

Reading

1 Answer the questions about Chapter Three.

What kind of fruit did Robinson find on the island?
Grapes and oranges

1 What did he use to make a bag for his fruit?

2 Why did he want to be near the sea?

3 Which home was good in all weather?

4 What was the weather like in September?

5 Why did he take a parrot home?

6 Why did he put three dead birds on a tree near his grain?

7 Why didn't he use his boat?

Grammar

2 Choose the right word in each sentence.

Today it is *rains* / *raining* on the island.
1 It *doesn't* / *isn't* usually rain much in June.
2 Robinson *teaches* / *is teaching* his parrot to speak every day.
3 He *has* / *is having* orange juice for breakfast this morning.
4 He *is being* / *is* at home today because the weather is bad.
5 He *wants* / *is wanting* to make a boat.
6 He *is working* / *works* today on his farm.
7 He *is liking* / *likes* his island now.

Internet Research and Speaking

2030 Agenda

Goal 2: *'End hunger, achieve food security and improved nutrition and promote sustainable agriculture'*

3 A **In Chapter Three, we read how Robinson Crusoe now has lots of things to eat on the island. This isn't true for everybody in the world. Search on the Internet for the following information.**

1 What began to happen in 2015?
2 How many people in the world suffer from hunger?
3 How many more people will be hungry by 2050 if we do nothing to change things?
4 Where do most of these people live?

3 B **Now talk to your partner and answer these questions.**

1 How often do you have a snack? What do you have?
2 Do you think it's important to have a big breakfast? Why? / Why not?
3 Who usually cooks at home?
4 What's your favourite food?
5 How much food do you throw away?

Pre-Reading Activity • Chapter Four

Vocabulary

4 **These are all words in Chapter Four. Read the sentences and write the words.**

	Things you wear.	C <u>LOTHE</u>S
1	You put these on your feet.	S _ _ _ _
2	You can travel on this at sea.	B _ _ _
3	It's white and you drink it.	M _ _ _
4	It's green and you find it in the garden.	G _ _ _ _
5	You use this part of your body to walk.	F _ _ _
6	A person you like.	F _ _ _ _ _
7	You use this to pay at the shops.	M _ _ _ _

Chapter Four

Savages

▶ 6 After many years on the island, I needed new clothes. I only had some shirts from the ship. There were also some coats, but it was hot to wear them. I made new clothes from my goats. I made a big hat and an umbrella because the sun was hot on my head. The umbrella was very difficult to make. When I was in Brazil, I knew some men near my plantation. They made umbrellas. I thought for a long time until I remembered how to make one. It wasn't a beautiful umbrella but I liked it. It could open and close… clever eh? It was good for both the sun and the rain. Then I made trousers and shoes. They weren't very nice but I had clothes again.

Now, life on the island was hard but good. I was never bored because I had a lot of work to do every day. I made a boat, a small boat this time. My old boat, the big one, was there on the beach where it was before. I couldn't do long voyages with the new boat because it was small; but I could go to the other part of the island with it by sea. I made a sail for my boat too, from one of the ship's sails. I put boxes at each end of the boat and put food and water in them. I took my gun with me too and my new umbrella. At first I did some short voyages but always stayed near the beach. Then, I was ready to visit all the island from the open sea. For this long voyage, I took a lot of bread, water and other food for some weeks. I also took two big coats for a bed.

I started my voyage on the 6th November. I travelled for many days and nights. Sometimes I went out to the open sea, and sometimes I travelled near the beach where possible. I stopped on a new beach. There was a hill behind it. I went up the hill and looked about.

From the hill, I could see the next part of the sea. It was different; it wasn't safe. The wind and the waves took everything out to sea. I stayed on this part of the island for two days because there was a lot of wind. Then, I started my voyage again. The beach was far from me now, and I felt the waves under the boat. The boat went up and down and the waves took it out to sea. I couldn't see the beach now. There wasn't any wind and it was difficult to get back to my island. I had a turtle to eat and some water… food for four or five days… but then what? There were no other islands near here and I couldn't get back to the beach.

I was happy on my island. I had everything I needed on my island. Why did I take my boat out and leave all that was good? It was the same old problem all the time. I never knew when I had a good life. I always wanted to change. Why? Why? Now I was at sea and I couldn't see my island.

Robinson now talks about the island as if it is his. He now has control of his life on the island.

Then, there was a little wind and it began to catch the sail. I worked hard with the sail to get back to my beautiful island. In the evening I was on the beach again. I sat down on the sand. I was tired but very happy. I found a little cave near the beach and slept there that night.

Next morning, I left my boat in this cave. I didn't want to go back home by sea. I took my gun, my hat and my umbrella and started walking back to my garden house. It was nice to be home again and I slept there that night. I woke up next morning to the words: 'Robin! Robin Crusoe!' For a second, I thought there was a person in my garden house. Then, I looked up… it was Poll my parrot. These were some of the words that he knew. Every evening, I taught him new words. He wasn't a person but I was happy to see him. Poll came to me and sat on my hand. I talked to him and told him about my days at sea. He said: 'Poor Robin Crusoe! How did you come here?' Then, I carried him home to my farm house.

The 30th September came again. Fifteen years before, when I first came to this island, I couldn't see any good here. Now I loved my life. I had forty goats and they gave me milk. With this milk I made butter and cheese. I had Poll to talk to. My dog was old and always sat at my feet, under the table. The two cats sat near me as well and waited for some food from my table.

These weren't the cats from the ship, but their children. The only thing I didn't have near me was my boat. It was in the cave on the other part of the island. I didn't know how to get it here. I didn't want to go out to sea again with those waves and the wind. But I wanted to go back to that part of the island. One day, I put on my hat, got my umbrella and walked to the hill above the beach where my boat was.

I went down to the beach and took out my boat, but I stayed near the beach. At night, I slept in my garden house. I did this a lot. I liked going out in my boat.

One morning, I came down to the beach and there was a man's footprint* in the sand. 'Eh?' I hear you ask. Think how I felt! I sat and looked at it for a long time. I listened. I looked about. I could hear nothing. I couldn't see anybody. I went back up the hill and looked... nobody. I went up and down the beach... nobody. I came back to the footprint. There it was. I could see it well in the sand, only one. After a long time, I went home to my garden house. I looked behind me when I walked home. I wasn't happy. I didn't want anybody on my island. I thought there was somebody behind every tree, waiting for me. I didn't sleep that night. I could hear all kinds of noises. Were they the noises I usually heard on the island? How did this person come to my island? There was no other boat near the beach. I thought of the two islands out at sea. You could only see them on a good day, because they weren't near. Did savages live there and come to my island sometimes? Did they know I was here? I thought about that footprint for days. After three days, I went back to the beach. Was it my footprint? But no, it wasn't. This foot was very big. My foot was small. After fifteen years, for the first time, I didn't feel safe on my island. I made a new wall for my house. Nobody could see it from the outside with this second wall.

Then, I put guns on the wall in different places, ready for anything or anybody. I had seven guns. I made this second wall in a month. There were also trees outside the wall so nobody could see my house. I wanted my goats to be safe too. I put them in two groups. I took them to different parts of the island. There was grass for them and lots of trees so nobody could find them.

Now, I didn't feel free to walk about my island. I only went to my

Daniel Defoe

Robinson is looking down at the beach from the hill and he sees five boats.

garden house or to my goats. I didn't go back to my boat in the cave on the beach. I didn't use my gun because I didn't want to make a noise. I often went up the hill to see if there was anybody on the beach below. I found a small cave on this hill and put some guns there too.

After a year, I thought it was safe to go and get my boat. I didn't want to leave it near the 'footprint beach' (my name for it). I carried it to my part of the island and put it in a cave. I stopped making things. I was sad. I only worked for my food now. Ten years came and went again, but I didn't feel free. It was December and I was busy with my grain and rice. I went out early one morning, with my hat and umbrella and my gun. It was hot. I went up the hill to look down at the beach. Eh? This time there wasn't a footprint in the sand. There were five boats on the beach! They were on the sand near the water. Whose boats were they? Were there savages about? How many were there? I sat in the cave on the hill and waited.

There was no noise. Then, hush! I could hear something. Some savages came out from behind the trees near the beach. There were a lot of them. I don't know how many. They went to their boats and went away. Phew! I came down to the beach and looked about. From up on the hill I could only see the boats. Now down here I could see everything! The beach was long and at one end I saw their fire* and near it some of their food. Oh! It can't be! A man's head! A hand! A foot! I ran back to my house behind my two walls and stayed there for days and days. I couldn't sleep at night. I could see the savages' picnic every time I closed my eyes. I didn't want to be their next dinner!

The savages were cannibals.

fire

Then, I had to go out again; for my goats, my grain, my grapes. I went up the hill every morning and looked for their boats but there weren't any. The months came and went. I began to forget the savages.

One night, there was a storm. I couldn't sleep. I was on my hammock in my farm house. Then, I heard the noise of a gun... and again... It couldn't be savages; they didn't have guns. I ran out of my house and up the hill. From there, I could see a ship at sea. It was difficult to see because it was far from my island. It went up and down with the wind and the waves. I made a big fire on the hill to help them see the island. I stayed there until morning. The storm stopped. The weather was nice again.

I looked out to sea. I could see a part of the ship above the water. The other part was at the bottom of the sea.

I took my boat and went to the ship. It was a Spanish ship. These ships usually went from South America to Spain. Was there anybody on the ship? A friend for me? There were people on the ship, but they were all dead at the bottom of the sea. I found a dog. It was hungry. I gave it food and water and took it back to my island. I also found some clothes and some money. I took the money, but I didn't need it on my island. I was sad. I wanted a friend not all this money!

After this, I felt bad for a long time. I remembered when I had friends. Now I only had Poll to talk to. I began to think about leaving my island after twenty-five years! It was March. The weather was bad. I stayed inside on my hammock and thought and slept. I didn't want to leave the island and go to the savages' country. I needed someone to tell me where to go. Someone who knew these places that I could sometimes see on a good day.

The next day, I went up the hill and looked down at the beach. The savages were back! They had three men with them. Three men they wanted to eat! One of them looked about. He was a young man. He didn't want to die. He saw the trees and started to run to them. The savages had the other two men. They couldn't catch this young man. He was fast. I watched from the hill. Then, I went down to help him. I found him behind a tree. I took him to my house. He thought he was my dinner! I gave him some food and water. He understood he was safe from the savages now. At last, I had a friend!

After-Reading Activities • Chapter Four

Reading

❶ Put the sentences about Chapter Four in the right order (A to H).

- **A** Robinson makes new clothes.
- **1** ☐ Robinson finds a friend.
- **2** ☐ Robinson sees a footprint in the sand.
- **3** ☐ Robinson goes to sea in a small boat.
- **4** ☐ The goats give Robinson milk.
- **5** ☐ A Spanish ship has problems in a storm near the island.
- **6** ☐ Poll speaks to Robinson.
- **7** ☐ Savages come to the island on five boats.

Vocabulary

❷ Match the pictures to the correct words.

a boat
b cave
c clothes
d ship
e parrot
f footprint

Writing

❸ Write sentence about Chapter Four with the words in exercise 2 and the past simple of the verbs in the box.

find - die - need - see - make - tell

1 .... 4 ....
2 .... 5 ....
2 .... 6 ....

Pre-Reading Activity • Chapter Five

Listening

▶ 7 **4 Listen to the start of Chapter Five and choose the right answer, A, B or C.**

Robinson called his new friend Friday because
- ☐ **A** he liked that day.
- ☑ **B** he came to the island on a Friday.
- ☐ **C** it was easy for Friday to remember.

1 Friday had
- ☐ **A** long legs and big feet.
- ☐ **B** long legs and small feet.
- ☐ **C** short legs and big feet.

2 Friday was about
- ☐ **A** twenty-seven years old.
- ☐ **B** thirty-six years old.
- ☐ **C** twenty-six years old.

3 Friday's eyes were
- ☐ **A** black.
- ☐ **B** brown.
- ☐ **C** blue.

4 Friday ate then slept for about
- ☐ **A** an hour and a half.
- ☐ **B** half an hour.
- ☐ **C** a quarter of an hour.

5 Friday didn't have any
- ☐ **A** teeth.
- ☐ **B** hair.
- ☐ **C** clothes.

6 They went back to the beach
- ☐ **A** the day after.
- ☐ **B** a week later.
- ☐ **C** after a year.

7 When they went to the beach, Robinson gave Friday
- ☐ **A** a gun.
- ☐ **B** a hat.
- ☐ **C** an umbrella.

Chapter Five

Friday

▶ 7 I was very happy to have a friend. I called him Friday because he came to my island on a Friday. He was a young man. He was tall with long legs and big feet. I think he was about twenty-six years old. It was difficult to know because he couldn't speak English. I used my hands to tell and show him things. He was happy to be safe from the savages and I understood that he wanted to be my slave. I had to teach him everything but I enjoyed it. I had somebody to talk to! He had a nice, happy face and big, brown eyes. His hair was long and black. He had a small nose and mouth. His teeth were very white.

After I gave him some water and bread, he slept for about half an hour. When he woke up, he came out of the cave to look for me. I was with my goats. He ran to me and showed me that he wanted to help me. He put his head at my feet to show me that he was my slave now. I was very happy for this. I needed a slave to help me with all the work. I began to speak to him and teach him some words. He learned his name, Friday. He also learned to call me 'Master*' and to say 'yes' and 'no'. I showed him the things I ate. He learned to drink milk and eat bread and liked them very much. I gave him some clothes because he didn't have any. We waited until the next day to go out again. Then, we went up the hill to look at the beach. We couldn't see

For Robinson it's normal that Friday becomes his slave, like what usually happened in the world at that time.

master the person who has a slave

any savages now. There were no boats on the beach. I gave Friday a gun and we went down to the beach.

8 When I saw the beach I felt really bad. There were heads and feet and hands everywhere. Friday wanted to eat them!

'No! No! Friday!' I said.

He looked at me with sad eyes.

'Don't worry, Friday,' I said. 'We can eat lots of other things, nice things!'

He didn't understand. I took him home and gave him some cheese.

'Yummy!' I said and put some cheese in my mouth.

He did the same. He was happy now.

Now I had to make a place for Friday to sleep. I got two sails and made a bedroom for him outside my cave. He was safe here because there was a big wall between his bedroom and the outside of my home. He was happy with his bedroom and his bed. I gave him a big coat for a bed and he slept well on it. I made a door between Friday's bedroom and my cave. He couldn't get into my cave at night because I closed the door and put my chair behind it. Every evening I took all the guns and put them in my room. But Friday was never a problem. He was a great slave and did everything for me.

'Don't worry, master. Friday do it,' he said when he saw I was tired. He was my son, not a slave. I was his father, not his master. He was a great student too and learned to speak very well. I had a beautiful life now on my island. I had everything I needed. There was only one problem… the savages.

I wanted Friday to understand that it wasn't good to eat men. There were other kinds of meat that were good to eat. I took him

Daniel Defoe

Robinson and Friday are making a big boat from a tree.

with me one day to get a goat for dinner. I got the goat with the gun.

When Friday heard the noise of the gun, his face was sad.

'Don't worry, Friday. Guns always make this noise,' I said.

We took the goat home and made it for dinner. First, I put some in my mouth and said: 'Yummy!'

Then, I gave some to Friday and he liked it. He wasn't a savage now; he was my slave, my son and my friend. He helped me with my grain and rice and I taught him to make bread. In a short time, Friday could do all the work for me. He knew a lot of words now and we had great conversations. I asked him about his country. He told me that his people were savages too.

'I came to this island many times with my people. Then those bad people took me and wanted to eat me. But you came and now I'm safe,' he said.

'But why did you come here?' I asked.

'To eat the bad men we caught, the men from other countries,' he said.

'Isn't it difficult to get home from here in your boats?' I asked.

'No, everybody gets home. The waves always take us back to our country,' said Friday.

I asked him lots about his country and his people. He told me there were some men with white beards there. They came four years before when their ship went to the bottom of the sea.

Robinson wants to meet these people because they're Europeans like him.

'Can you take me to these men with white beards, Friday?'

'Yes, but we need a big boat.'

We found a good tree and started to make our boat. I was excited. I wanted to meet these men.

Were they some of the men on the Spanish ship? The ship I visited after the storm? He told me there were seventeen of these men in his country.

After twenty-seven years on this island, it was now possible to leave. I had Friday to take me to these Europeans in his country. He knew the sea well, the wind and the waves. He knew the right time to go.

We made the boat together. We made it near the water this time. I told him about my life. I taught him to use a gun and I gave him a knife too. He was very happy with these things. I told him about Europe and a lot about England. He told me that in his country, his people were nice to the Europeans. That was good! I was worried about those savages!

One beautiful morning, we went up the hill. Friday looked out to sea and said:

'Hey! Look master! My country!' He was very excited.

'Would you like to be there?' I asked.

'Oh yes!' he said. 'But not to be a savage. I want to tell them about my new life. I want to teach them all the new things I know, master. And you'll come with me. They'll be happy to meet you. You can teach them lots of new things.'

'Well, we have to finish our boat!' I said.

We finished our boat in a month after a lot of hard work. It was big. I made sails for the new boat with the old sails from the ship. I worked on these sails for two months. Then I taught Friday to use them. The rain came. I waited for the good weather again. We took our boat up the river to a safe place. We waited for November or December to come to start our voyage.

When the weather was fine again, I started to put some food in boxes for the voyage.

One morning, I told Friday to go down to the beach to get a turtle. After some minutes he was back.

'Oh master! Oh bad!' he said.

'What's bad Friday?' I asked.

'Three boats on the beach, master! Three!'

'Don't worry, Friday. We'll think of something,' I said.

But Friday was very worried; worried that these savages were here to find him and eat him.

'The savages won't take you from me, Friday. I'll die first!'

'No, they'll die, not you!' said Friday.

'Yes, of course! We'll use our guns. They'll all die! Take me to them, Friday!'

We took our guns and went up the hill. From here I could see that there were twenty-one savages on the beach with three boats. In one of these boats, there were three other men. They were the savages' dinner! There were trees near the beach. I told Friday to follow me to the trees. We stayed near each other and didn't say a word. We watched the savages from behind the trees. They were near their fire. There were only two men in the boat now. One of these wasn't a savage but a man with a white beard, a European! It was time to do something, before they ate him too.

'Now, Friday!' I said 'Do what I do! Use your gun!'

The savages heard the noise but they didn't run. They looked about. They couldn't see us. They didn't know what to do. The first time, five savages died, then four, then six, then two. We ran out from

Daniel Defoe

The Spanish man and Friday's father are going back to tell the Europeans to come and live on Robinson's island.

behind the trees. Four savages got into a boat. I ran to the man with the white beard to help him. I gave him some water and some bread.

Then I went to the other man. He was happy there were no savages to eat him now. I gave him some bread and water too. Then, I called Friday to speak to him because he was from his country. When Friday saw the man, he said: 'Hooray! Hooray!' and danced about. I couldn't understand why. Then, he told me:

'Master, this is my father!'

I was very happy for Friday and his father. We brought him and the Spanish man home. That night there was a lot of wind. I thought about the boat with the savages in it. Did they get back to their island? Anyhow, after that night, no savages ever came to the island again.

We made a room for the Spanish man and Friday's father with some of the ship's sails. They slept well there. I had a lot of people on my island now, and I was master of them all! We spoke a lot together. The Spanish man told me that he lived with sixteen other Europeans. He said that they didn't have a good life there.

'Tell them to come here and we can make a big boat together and go to Brazil or Spain,' I said.

'They can live well here until we're ready to leave the island.'

We used the next six months to work on my farm. We needed a lot of rice and grain now for all these people. Everybody worked hard. In October, the Spanish man and Friday's father left on a boat to go and tell the others about my island.

'Goodbye! Tell them, I'll wait for them. I'll give them a good life here,' I said. 'Then we can all leave this island together and go back to Europe or America. Hooray!'

After-Reading Activities • Chapter Five

Reading

1 **Are these sentences about Chapter Five right (A) or wrong (B)?**

	A	B
Friday slept in Robinson's bedroom.	☐	☑
1 Robinson learned to speak Friday's language.	☐	☐
2 Friday said it was easy to get to his country by boat.	☐	☐
3 There were twenty Europeans in Friday's country.	☐	☐
4 Friday's brother came to the island with some savages.	☐	☐
5 The savages didn't have guns.	☐	☐
6 The Spanish man went back to Spain to see his friends.	☐	☐
7 Robinson said goodbye to the Spanish man in October.	☐	☐

Writing

2 **You're Robinson. Write a letter to the Spanish man's friends. In your letter, talk about your life on the island:**

- your houses
- your food
- your animals
- what you do every day
- Friday

Grammar A1 MOVERS

3 Choose the right words (A, B or C) to complete the text about Chapter Five.

Robinson was **(0)** ......*very*...... happy to have Friday on his island and Friday was happy to be safe **(1)** .... the savages. Robinson made a bedroom for **(2)** .... outside the cave. Friday **(3)** .... never a problem and he did everything for Robinson. He also learned to speak English very **(4)** .... He told Robinson that some men with white beards lived in his country. Robinson wanted to meet **(5)** .... so they made a boat to go there.

0	**A** much	**(B) very**	**C** too
1	**A** by	**B** to	**C** from
2	**A** him	**B** his	**C** he
3	**A** were	**B** was	**C** had
4	**A** good	**B** well	**C** fine
5	**A** they	**B** their	**C** them

Pre-Reading Activity • Chapter Six

Listening

▶9 **4 Listen to the start of Chapter Six and put the words in each sentence in the right order.**

I / sea / to / the / ran / at / look.
I ran to look at the sea.

1 see / could / I / boat / near / a / beach / the.
2 men / my / from / were / these / country.
3 eleven / there / men / were.
4 men / had / these / guns.
5 bad / sleeping / men / under/ trees / the/ are / the.
6 took / me / these / from / my / men / ship.

Chapter Six

Going Home

▶ 9 We waited for Friday's father and the Spanish man to come back. Then, after eight days, Friday came to me one morning and said:

'Master! Master! They're coming!'

I ran to look at the sea. I could see a boat near the beach. It wasn't the boat Friday's father left with.

'Are they friends, master?' asked Friday.

'I don't know, Friday. Come with me. We'll go up the hill to see.'

We went up the hill and looked out at sea. There was a big ship. It was far from the beach, but I could see it was an English ship. The boat near the beach was their boat. Was I happy or sad? I didn't know. These men were from my country; but what was their business here, near my island? English ships didn't usually come to these parts. There was something wrong in all this, but I didn't know what.

I saw their boat on the beach now. There were eleven men. The hands and feet of three men weren't free and they were on the sand, face down. They were their prisoners*. Friday was with me and asked:

'Master, are these English savages, ready to eat those three men?'

'No, Friday, but they're bad men,' I answered. 'Those men are their prisoners.'

prisoner a person who isn't free

Robinson Crusoe

These men had guns; the savages didn't. I didn't know what to do. They left the three prisoners on the beach and went to look at the island. We stayed on the hill above my house. Then, when it was about two o'clock, we went home and I got my guns. I gave some to Friday too. He was good with a gun and I needed his help. It was very hot now.

'Come Friday,' I said. 'The bad men are sleeping under the trees.'

We went to the beach to the three prisoners. I called to them in English:

'Don't worry, I'm a friend,' I said, when I was near them. 'I'm English and I want to help you.'

'I was captain of that ship out there,' said one man. 'Then, these men took my ship from me. Now I'm their prisoner with these two good men you can see with me. They want to leave us on this island to die.'

'We can catch them while they're sleeping. They'll be your prisoners and you'll have your ship again,' I said.

'Thank you, my friend. We'll help you catch them. Tell us what to do,' said the captain.

'OK! But you have to do two things for me. First, for the time we're on this island, you'll do what I say. Second, when you're captain again, you'll take me and my man, Friday, to England.'

'Of course!' said the captain, 'and I won't ask you to pay.'

'Great!' I said. 'Now, take these three guns. We have to be quick before they wake up.'

We went to the trees and soon you could hear the noise of our guns. Two men died. We told the others: 'Choose to die or to work for your captain again on the ship.' They all wanted to go back to the ship, of course!

'OK! But for now, on this island, you're my prisoners,' I said.

Friday and the captain's two men took the prisoners and watched them. The captain and I now had time to talk. I told him about my life on the island. When he heard about all the things I did every day, he said:

'You're a clever man, Robinson Crusoe.'

Then I took him and his men home. I gave them some milk, bread and cheese. They also ate some grapes. Then we spoke about the ship. There were twenty-six men on the ship. They didn't know their captain was a free man again.

'How can we get my ship from all these men?' the captain asked me.

'First we'll go to the boat on the beach and take all the guns there. Then we'll use the boat to make a fire,' I said.

Then, we heard the noise of a gun from the ship.

'They're calling their friends,' said the captain.

'And when their friends don't answer, some of them will come here to look for them,' I said.

Soon after, we saw them coming. There were ten men in a small boat. They had guns. We waited for them behind the trees. We could see their faces. The captain told me that some of these men were very bad.

'Don't worry,' I said. 'They don't know we're waiting for them.' Friday took the prisoners to a cave. He left them some food and water.

'I'll come back soon,' said Friday. 'Be good!'

The men from the ship came onto the beach with their boat. They looked for the other boat, but couldn't find it of course. They called their friends. Nobody answered. They thought their men were all dead. They went back into their boat to go back to the ship. Then, three men stayed in the boat and the others came back onto the beach. They went into the trees to look for their friends. This was difficult for us. Now, there were seven men on the island and three in the boat. We couldn't attack them all together.

We could only wait and watch. The seven men went up the hill and called their friends, but nobody answered. They sat under a tree to have a rest. We waited. Then, they went back down the hill to the beach.

'What are they doing?' the captain asked.

'I think they're going back to the boat to go to the ship,' I said.

The captain was very worried by this.

'What about my ship? We'll never leave this island now!' he said.

'Don't worry. Listen to me,' I said.

I told Friday to go up the hill and call out to the men on the boat. When they heard him, they were excited. They thought it was one of their friends. They ran up the beach. They came to a river. Friday called again. They called their men in the boat at the beach. They told them to come with the boat up the river. Two men came with the boat, one stayed on the beach. Friday called again. They couldn't see him. There were trees all around them. They were far from the beach now. They could only hear Friday. Now was the time to catch them. Our first prisoner was the man on the beach. He was easy to catch because there were five of us and only one of him! Then we got the two men in the boat. That was easy too. Friday called again. Then, one of the captain's men called from a different

Daniel Defoe

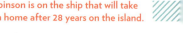
Robinson is on the ship that will take him home after 28 years on the island.

hill. Now the men didn't know where to go. They went up and down hill and were soon very tired. We waited in the dark, ready to catch them. They came back to their boat after many hours.

'Where are our two men?' we heard them ask.

'With us!' I said.

Then we ran at them. After an hour, two very bad men were dead and the others were our prisoners. Our next job was to get the ship. The captain spoke to the prisoners.

'Help me get my ship back and you won't die,' he said.

'Of course!' they all said.

They weren't very bad men. They were sorry and wanted to help the captain. Friday and I stayed on the island. The captain and his men went to the ship at midnight. Some men died. At two o'clock, Friday and I heard the ship's gun seven times. This told us that the captain had his ship again.

'Hooray!' I said, and danced up and down the beach with Friday. 'It's time to go home and our ship is waiting for us!' Then we slept, because we were very tired. Next morning, the captain came. We went up the hill to look out to sea.

'Look, dear Robinson. There's the ship that will take you and your man, Friday, home!'

I wanted to say a lot of things, but no words came. Then, the captain gave me some things from his ship. He gave me sugar and lots of other nice things to eat. He also gave me clothes: six clean new shirts, two pairs of shoes, a hat, and a very good pair of trousers and a jacket. I was very happy, but at first it was difficult for me to wear them after many years with my island clothes.

Daniel Defoe

Then we spoke about our prisoners. We left two men on the island. The others came with us. Twenty-eight years on this island and now it was time to go home. I took Friday with me of course, and also my umbrella, my hat, my parrot and the money I had.

Before leaving, I showed the two men how to live on the island. I also left a letter for the Spanish men and told the others to be good to them. I showed the men my goats and how to get milk to make cheese and butter. I showed them my grain and told them how to make bread.

'Thank you,' they said. 'We'll have a good life here.'

We started our voyage home next morning, on the 19th December 1686. After a long voyage, we came to England, on 11th June 1687, thirty-five years after I first left my father and mother. Nobody knew me. I went to my home in Yorkshire but my mother and father were dead. I didn't have much money now, but the master of the ship was good to me. The captain told him how I helped him get his ship back. The master was very happy and gave me £200.

With this money I went to Lisbon with my man, Friday. In Lisbon, after all these years, I met my old friend the Portuguese captain. At first he didn't know me. I spoke about how he took Xury and I on his ship after finding us at sea. Then, he remembered me and my problems with the pirates. He didn't work between Brazil and Africa now, but he told me that my plantation was great.

'The friends you left in Brazil work every day on your plantation. It's there, waiting for you,' said the old captain.

I was very happy to hear this. I wrote to my friends in Brazil. They were excited to hear I wasn't dead after all this time. They told me

---

During Robinson's time on the island, two important events happened in London:

The Great Plague of London in 1665 and The Great Fire of London in 1666.

that they had a lot of money for me from the sugar plantation.

I was a rich man! They sent me money and other things on ships from Brazil. I now had £5000 and my sugar plantation in Brazil gave me £1000 a year. I gave some money to the old Portuguese captain. With this money he lived the last years of his life well. I didn't know what to do with all this money; where to put it or who to give it to. I wanted to go back to England, but I had some business to do. I wrote letters to my friends in Brazil. Then, I sent my bags to England by ship, but this time I didn't want to travel by sea. I don't know why. I chose a ship, then didn't go. Weeks later, they told me the ship never got to England and all the people on it died at sea. After this, I chose to go by road also because I had a lot of time to travel. I didn't have a job or a family. I could do what I wanted.

I left Lisbon with my man, Friday, and some other people. First, we rode to Madrid. We visited the city, then left near the end of October. We met lots of people on the road. They told us that there was a lot of snow in the French mountains. We came to the next town near the mountains. It was very cold and there was a lot of snow. It was very difficult to travel on the roads. We stayed in this town for twenty days. We waited for the snow to stop. We chose a different road. There was snow but not much. Sometimes there were animals. Our guns were always ready. We started on 15th November and rode for many days. We could hear animals in the night but we couldn't see them.

Then, one day we met a bear*. We were on our horses when this big bear came out from behind the trees. Friday saw it and said:

'Oh Master, don't worry. I'll play with the bear!'

Before I could speak, Friday ran to the bear. The bear saw Friday.

bear see page 69

Daniel Defoe

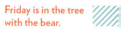

Friday is in the tree with the bear.

Friday called the animal, then ran to a tree and went up it fast. The bear came after him. Now they were both up the tree. Friday was at the end of a long branch*.

'Come Mr. Bear, come and dance,' said Friday.

Friday danced up and down on the branch. The bear had big problems.

'Oh Mr. Bear. Please dance with me!' said Friday.

The bear didn't know what to do. It was difficult to stay on the branch. We watched Friday and the bear. It was very funny. Friday was happy with his game. After some time, he got the bear with his gun.

Then, we started travelling again. After many days and nights in the mountains, we got to France. Then on 14th January, we came to Dover, in England. I was home! I wrote to my friends in Brazil to tell them I didn't want to come back. They were sad, but happy too, because they bought my plantation from me and it wasn't expensive.

For the next seven years, I lived with my dead brother's sons and sent them to school. One of them liked the sea and I gave him a ship. In 1694, I travelled on his ship to my island to visit the Spanish men there. I stayed for 20 days. I was happy to see that they lived well on my island. Yes, my island, because before, there was nothing; now they had everything they needed, thanks to me.

Today Dover is a major port town facing the English Channel and just 21 miles from the French port of Calais. It's the closest English port to Europe.

branch part of a tree

After-Reading Activities • Chapter Six

Reading

1 Complete these questions about Chapter Six with a word or expression from the box. Then, match the questions to the right answers.

> where • when • how much • why • how • ~~what kind of~~ • what time • how many

- [d] *What kind of* ship came to the island?
1. [ ] .... did Robinson and Friday go home to get their guns?
2. [ ] .... prisoners did the English men have?
3. [ ] .... did Friday take the prisoners?
4. [ ] .... did Robinson leave the island to go home?
5. [ ] .... money did his friends in Brazil send him?
6. [ ] .... did Robinson send his bags from Lisbon to England?
7. [ ] .... did Friday go up the tree?

a to a cave.
b by ship.
c 19th December 1686.
~~d~~ an English ship.
e three.
f to get the bear.
g about two o'clock.
h £5000.

Writing

2 You're Robinson. Write about what you do after visiting the Spanish men on your island. Talk about:

• where you go   • what you do   • who you meet

Grammar

3 **Read about *Robinson Crusoe*. Choose the right word, A, B or C for each space.**

Robinson is a young man and he likes ....*travelling*..... . First, he goes **(1)** .... London. Then, he travels on a ship to Africa. The first time, the voyage goes **(2)** .... The second time, some **(3)** .... take the ship and Robinson's money. He works **(4)** .... for the captain. The captain sends Xury and Robinson to catch **(5)** .... fish. Robinson kicks a man into the water. Then, Robinson and Xury travel in the boat. A Portuguese captain finds **(6)** .... and takes Robinson and Xury on his ship to Brazil. **(7)** .... Brazil, Robinson buys a sugar plantation and makes **(8)** .... of money. Then, he wants to travel to Africa again to get slaves for the plantation. He **(9)** .... gets to Africa because there is a storm. The waves take him to a desert island. **(10)** .... on the ship dies. Only Robinson gets to the island. He lives on this island. **(11)** .... years. In the end **(12)** .... English ship takes him home.

	A travelling	**B** travel	**C** travels
1	**A** at	**B** to	**C** in
2	**A** good	**B** very	**C** well
3	**A** slaves	**B** pirates	**C** savages
4	**A** much	**B** many	**C** hard
5	**A** an	**B** any	**C** some
6	**A** them	**B** you	**C** her
7	**A** On	**B** In	**C** At
8	**A** many	**B** very	**C** lots
9	**A** doesn't	**B** never	**C** not
10	**A** Everybody	**B** Somebody	**C** Anybody
11	**A** from	**B** for	**C** to
12	**A** the	**B** an	**C** a

Speaking 21st Century Skills

4 **Work in pairs. Talk about these questions.**
- What's your favourite part of the story?
- What did you like about Robinson?
- What didn't you like about Robinson?

Focus on...

Daniel Defoe (1660-1731)

Daniel Defoe – nobody is sure when and where he was born, but it was probably about 1660 in London. He was an English novelist, pamphleteer, journalist and trader.

1670

Family and Education
His father was called James Foe. Daniel added 'De' to his surname in his 30s to make it sound more important. His mother, Annie, died when Defoe was only 10 years old. He went to school in Surrey and London and was a good student.

1684

Marriage
Defoe married Mary Tuffley in 1684. She came from a rich family which helped Defoe who always had money problems. They were together for 47 years and had 8 children.

Friend
Defoe was a good friend of William III who became king in 1688. He helped the king a lot and became his secret agent in 1689.

1695

Working life
At first Defoe was a trader and people bought clothes and wine from him both in England and abroad. Then, he left England for a short time when he had money problems. He went to Lisbon and Cadiz where people bought wine from him. In 1695, he came back to England and opened a factory in Essex.

Writing Success
Defoe was very interested in politics and business and wrote the first of many political pamphlets in 1683. He didn't start writing books until he was almost 60 years old. Between 1719 and 1724, he wrote his most famous novels *Robinson Crusoe* (1719) and *Moll Flanders* (1724). His many works cover various subjects like crime, religion, marriage, psychology and the supernatural.

Robinson Crusoe and his companion Friday with their animals.

1731

Final Years
Defoe had money problems all his life and when he died in 1731, he had almost no money left. He's buried in Islington, London.

Focus on...

Atlantic Slave Trade*

The Atlantic Slave Trade started in the 16th century. People went to Africa to buy slaves. Then they put them on their ships and took them to America. People in the *New World* bought these slaves to work on their plantations.

Atlantic Travel

The Atlantic Slave Trade began after countries from the *Old World* (Europe, Africa and Asia) started to do business with the *New World* (North America and South America) Before the 15th century they didn't know how to make a ship to go from the *Old World* to the *New World*. It was difficult with the waves and the wind in the Atlantic Ocean. Then, they learned to make good ships that could do this kind of long voyage. Between 1600 and 1800, lots of ships went from Africa to America.

The people who worked on these ships saw new countries and learned new things about these people. European countries were very interested in travelling to the *New World* because they wanted to find new business outside Europe. They wanted to make money and be rich. Many countries had ships which travelled to the *New World* and the men on the ships came from lots of different countries; Portugal, Spain, England, Italy, France and Holland.

16th, 17th and 18th Centuries

People talk about the *First and Second Atlantic Systems*. In the *First System*, most of the people who did business with slaves were Portuguese. They bought their slaves in Africa and took them to Portuguese people who now lived in South America. Then Portugal stopped this business because they were partners with Spain and Spain didn't do slave trading. Other countries took their business and the *Second System* started.
In the *Second Atlantic System*, a lot of English, Dutch and French did slave trading. They sent a lot of their slaves to Caribbean countries and Brazil. The slave trade was slow in the 16th century. In the 17th century this business got more popular. The 18th century was the time when they sent lots and lots of slaves to America. England was a very big slave trader in the 18th century. Then in 1808 Britain and America banned* slave trading.

Triangular (△) Trade

The first part of this kind of trade was between Europe and Africa. Europeans took things to Africa for the people to buy. Some African masters gave the Europeans slaves because they wanted guns and other things from factories that they couldn't find in Africa.
In the second part of this triangular trade, the Europeans took African slaves to the *New World* where people bought them to work on their plantations.
In the last part of the triangle, people in the *New World* took the slaves and gave the Europeans things from the plantations, for example, sugar.

Task

Look on the internet and discover:
- Which parts of the *New World* they took slaves to in the 16th, 17th and 18th centuries.
- What kind of work the slaves did.

trade business   **ban** stop

Focus on...

Robinson Crusoe in the 20th and 21st Centuries

Everybody, all over the world, knows about the book *Robinson Crusoe*. People love to read about how a man can live on a desert island for many years and learn to do lots of things. There are films, TV programmes, cartoons and video games about Robinson Crusoe. Here are some of them.

Cinema

In the 1950s they made the film, *Adventures of Robinson Crusoe*, in Mexico. They made it both in Spanish and English. During filming, they always had their guns ready for wild animals that lived in those parts of Mexico. When they finished making the film they showed it in New York for the first time in 1954.

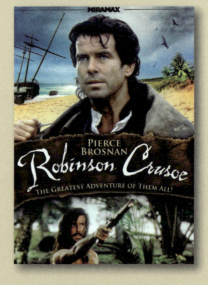

In 1997, there was the American/Australian film *Robinson Crusoe*, with the actor Pierce Brosnan as Robinson. Some things are different from Daniel Defoe's book. In the film, Robinson is Scottish, not English. In both the film and the book, Robinson lives on a desert island. At the end of the film, Friday dies and Crusoe goes back to Scotland to be with his wife, Mary. In the book, Friday goes home with Crusoe.

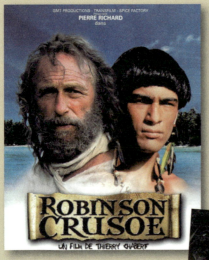

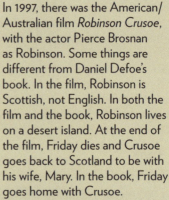

Another film which takes some parts from Defoe's book is the 2000 film *Cast Away* with the actor, Tom Hanks. It is about an American man, Chuck Noland. He has to stay on a desert island after his plane comes down in the sea. All the other people on the plane die. Chuck has to learn to live on this island and it is very different from his life in the United States. Lots of boxes that were on the plane come to the island with the waves. Chuck opens them on the island. The things are difficult to use because they aren't tools, but videos and other modern things. This isn't the same as in Defoe's book. Robinson finds good things on the ship to help him live on the island. Chuck doesn't have a man called Friday to talk to. He talks to a ball he calls 'Wilson'. In the end, he goes back to the United States and finds that his girlfriend has a husband and a daughter. He has to start a new life.

Cartoons

In the 1990s, there was a funny French cartoon called *Robinson Sucroe*. In the cartoon, Robinson works for a newspaper but he isn't very good at writing. He wants to go to a desert island and write about what he does every week. They leave him on an island but there are French and English pirates on it. Robinson finds a new friend called *Mercredi* (Wednesday). Robinson writes about his life every week but nobody likes his stories. Wednesday writes adventure stories for him. They are very good and he gives them to Robinson to send to the newspaper. Everybody at the newspaper likes these stories and nobody knows that Wednesday is the person who writes them.

Task

Complete this table. Write the things that are the same and different from Defoe's book.

	Same	Different
Robinson Crusoe (1997)		
Cast Away		
Robinson Sucroe		

Test Yourself

Choose A, B, or C to complete the sentences about *Robinson Crusoe*.

At the start of the story, Robinson is
A ☐ 20 years old. B ☑ 18 years old. C ☐ 25 years old.

1. In Africa, Robinson is the slave of
   A ☐ a savage. B ☐ a pirate. C ☐ a business man.

2. On the island, Robinson eats
   A ☐ bananas. B ☐ apples. C ☐ grapes.

3. On his farm he has
   A ☐ sheep. B ☐ horses. C ☐ goats.

4. He learns to make
   A ☐ bread. B ☐ biscuits. C ☐ ice cream.

5. His friend's name is
   A ☐ Wednesday. B ☐ Friday. C ☐ Sunday.

6. He leaves the island after
   A ☐ 25 years. B ☐ 27 years. C ☐ 28 years.

7. He leaves the island with
   A ☐ his dog. B ☐ his cat. C ☐ his parrot.

8. While he was on the island, his friends in Brazil
   A ☐ forgot him. B ☐ wrote to him. C ☐ worked on his plantation.

9. After his visit to Lisbon, he goes back to England
   A ☐ by road. B ☐ by sea. C ☐ by plane.

10. When he's in England he
    A ☐ finds a wife. B ☐ stays with his brother. C ☐ helps his brother's children.

Syllabus

Level A1

Verb forms and tenses

Present Continuous
Present Simple
Past simple (regular/irregular verbs)
Will for offers and with future meaning
Can / could (past simple)
Imperatives
Have to
Would like + infinitive
Common phrasal verbs
There is / there are

Sentence types

Two clauses with *so, before, after, when*
Direct speech + subject/verb inversion
Like/love/hate + ing form

Young Adult ELI Readers

STAGE 1 Sir Arthur Conan Doyle, *A Study in Scarlet*
Jonathan Swift, *Gulliver's Travels*
Sir Arthur Conan Doyle, *The Hound of the Baskervilles*
Daniel Defoe, *Robinson Crusoe*

STAGE 2 Shakespeare, *Hamlet Prince of Denmark*
Charles Dickens, *Great Expectations*
William Shakespeare, *Romeo and Juliet*
Bram Stoker, *Dracula*
William Shakespeare, *A Midsummer Night's Dream*
Robert Louis Stevenson, *The Strange Case of Dr Jekyll and Mr Hyde*
Jerome K. Jerome, *Three Men in a Boat*
John Buchan, *Thirty-Nine Steps*

STAGE 3 Charlotte Brontë, *Jane Eyre*
Jane Austen, *Pride and Prejudice*
Oscar Wilde, *The Picture of Dorian Gray*
William Shakespeare, *Macbeth*
Jane Austen, *Sense and Sensibility*
Edith Wharton, *The Age of Innocence*
Charles Dickens, *A Christmas Carol*
Wilkie Collins, *The Woman in White*
Anonymous, *Beowulf*
Robert Louis Stevenson, *Kidnapped*
Elizabeth Ferretti, *The Earthkeepers*
Thomas Hardy, *Tess of the d'Ubervilles*
George Orwell, *1984*

STAGE 4 James Joyce, *Dubliners*
Mary Shelley, *Frankenstein*
Henry James, *The Turn of the Screw*
Emily Brontë, *Wuthering Heights*
Edgar Allan Poe, *Stories of Mystery and Suspense*
Charles and Mary Lamb, *Tales from Shakespeare*
Charles Dickens, *A Tale of Two Cities*
Hermann Melville, *Moby Dick*
Jane Austen, *Emma*
Nathaniel Hawthorne, *The Scarlet Letter*
E.M. Forster, *A Passage to India*

STAGE 5 Virginia Woolf, *Mrs Dalloway*
Francis Scott Fitzgerald, *The Great Gatsby*

STAGE 6 Joseph Conrad, *Heart of Darkness*
J. Borsbey & R. Swan, Editors, *A Collection of First World War Poetry*
Oscar Wilde, *The Importance of Being Earnest*